872 0 P9-DDD-933

BY MY BROTHER'S SIDE

Tiki and Ronde Barber with Robert Burleigh
Illustrated by Barry Root

A PAULA WISEMAN BOOK

Simon & Schuster Books for Young Readers
NEW YORK   LONDON   TORONTO   SYDNEY

SIMON & SCHUSTER BOOKS FOR YOUNG READERS
An imprint of Simon & Schuster Children's Publishing Division
1230 Avenue of the Americas, New York, New York 10020
Book design by Dan Potash
The text for this book is set in Meridien.
The illustrations for this book are rendered in watercolor and gouache.
Manufactured in the United States of America
2 4 6 8 10 9 7 5 3 1
Library of Congress Cataloging-in-Publication Data • Barber, Tiki. • By my brother's
side / Tiki and Ronde Barber with Robert Burleigh ; illustrated by Barry Root. p. cm. "A
Paula Wiseman Book." Summary: Introduces twin brothers Tiki and Ronde Barber, who
worked hard to overcome obstacles and became National Football League stars, one as
running back for the New York Giants, the other as cornerback for the Tampa Bay
Buccaneers. ISBN 0-689-86559-7 • 1. Barber, Tiki, 1975-—Juvenile literature. 2. Barber,
Ronde, 1975-—Juvenile literature. 3. Football players—United States—Biography—
Juvenile literature. 4. Brothers—United States—Biography—Juvenile literature.
[1. Barber, Tiki, 1975- 2. Barber, Ronde, 1975- 3. Football players. 4. African
Americans—Biography.] I. Barber, Ronde, 1975- II. Burleigh, Robert. III. Root, Barry, ill.
IV. Title. GV939.A1 B364 2004 • 796.332'092'2—dc22 • 2003013130

Verizon is committed to being America's Literacy Champion by
orchestrating the fight for a more literate America through
grassroots campaigns and collaborative efforts that raise
community awareness, increase funding and resources, and
support a wide diversity of literacy programs across the country.
For more information about literacy and how you can join in
making a difference, please visit www.verizonreads.net.

Simon & Schuster Children's Publishing and the authors are proud supporters of Verizon Reads.

For AJ and Chason—T. B.

To my three roses, and to my family,
who helped me get to where I am today—R. B.

To Sam and Ben—B. R.

The authors and publisher gratefully acknowledge the assistance
of Mark Lepselter in creating this book.

It was summertime at last. School was out, and baseball season was in full swing. Once Tiki and Ronde finished their chores, they could play until dinnertime. The twins rode their bikes all over town. So just before lunch off they went—side by side, as was the case in pretty much everything they did.

Today they wanted to show their friend Jason a new secret place to ride bikes, a large open lot where workers were building a store. And since it was Saturday, the workers were gone.

"Betcha can't," said Jason.

"Can too," Ronde shot back. "Watch this, you guys."

As Tiki and Jason watched, Ronde slowly rode his dirt bike up and along the steep edge. Whoa, there! Ronde thought. Easy does it. The bike zigged and zagged and bounced—but Ronde steadied himself and held on.

"See," said Ronde. "Now you try if you're so good!"

Well, I'll show them, Tiki thought. He rode his bike to the far side of the huge dirt pile, and he popped a wheelie. Then he started up the hill. He stood high on the pedals, pushing with all his might. The bike wheels spun wildly, spitting up dirt.

Then the loose dirt on the hill's edge suddenly gave way. Tiki toppled sideways. Over the handlebars. Down . . . down . . . burnout.

He lay there, blinking. His head was reeling, but his knee hurt much more. Ronde and Jason dropped their bikes and ran up the hill. The boys leaned over Tiki.

Ronde pointed. "It's bleeding bad. I even see something white. I think it's . . . the bone!"

Jason put his hand over his eyes. "I don't want to look," he said. "We'd better get your mom—quick."

In the doorway Dr. Myers was whispering. "He needs lots of rest, Mrs. Barber."

Tiki called from his bed, "Mom, I'm bored, bored, BORED!"

Tiki's mother looked the doctor in the eye. "What about his leg, Doctor? Will he be able to run—like Ronde and the other kids?" For a moment she remembered when the twins were born smaller than most babies and how the doctor at the hospital had told her to take special care of them. She had thought then, like now, that no matter what, the boys would always have each other.

"It's a serious injury," Dr. Myers answered. "I'm not sure he will ever play sports again."

Mrs. Barber glanced at her son. "Please, let's not tell him anything like that," she said as she and the doctor walked slowly toward the front of the house. On the way to the door Ronde raced past them—"Hi, Mom"—heading to the boys' room.

But when their mother returned to the boys' room, the twins were gone.
She hurried to the back door. Tiki's crutch was on the kitchen floor. Their mother looked out the window and saw Ronde on the street, tossing a baseball to his brother, who was hobbling and hopping on one leg—but still managing to catch and throw the ball!

"Inside—at once! Both of you."

Tiki groaned. "Mom—there's an All-Star baseball game tonight. The team needs me."

"Yeah, Mom, I haven't ever played without Tiki. He's the fastest guy we have. Can't he even—"

"No," she said firmly. Then she turned to Tiki. "And as for you, Buster, Ronde will have to play for both of you. You're resting—for as long as it takes."

Ronde broke in. "Don't give up, Tiki. I'll hit one out tonight—for you and for me."

Tiki glanced up. "Really? Will you?"

"Promise," Ronde said with a grin. "For both of us."

July was long and hot. Whenever Ronde would go out to play baseball, Tiki would say, "Maybe I could just—"

"Not today," Tiki's mother would respond. And he knew that she meant it.

In the afternoon Ronde and Tiki sat in their room, talking brother to brother. The wall was filled with pictures: Bo Jackson, Michael Jordan, Walter Payton. And above the dresser was a picture of the twins—smiling, holding a trophy.

Ronde pointed to the photo. "Remember that game?"

"Do I ever!" Tiki moved his raised leg to the other pillow.

They loved to replay that special game in their minds. The county "Super Bowl." Pee Wee Leaguers. The Cave Spring Vikings. Their funny purple uniforms.

"Remember what Coach always said? 'Ronde is number 21 and Tiki is 22—because R comes before T, and this is how I can tell you apart!'"

Both boys burst out laughing. "And remember that great big kid on the Browns?" Tiki said. "I thought he'd run over us like a truck."

"Me too. But 'the bigger they are, the harder they fall.' Just ask Coach Mike."

"And the field. When I'd run for a long touchdown, I thought I'd never reach the goal line!"

"But you did. And we stuck together—and won. Remember the song they played over the loudspeaker afterward?" Ronde asked him.

"'We Are the Champions.' I can still hear it."

August was better. Just a little.

Baseball season was winding down, and for Tiki it was still the longest summer he could remember. Ronde dug in at the plate. Tiki sat in the dugout with his leg stretched straight out, cheering on his brother.

Ronde rode his bike. Tiki sat under a tree, waiting for his brother to come around the block one more time.

Ronde practiced his sprints. Tiki watched, counting the weeks until football practice would begin.

Ronde walked fast. Tiki limped behind.
"Come on, Tiki. You can do it. I know you can.
We're supposed to meet Chris in five minutes."
"I'm trying. Wait up."
"You know I won't leave you behind."

Tiki's mother would tell him stories about when the boys were very little and how the doctor had told her they shouldn't ever play too hard.

"You two were never the biggest for your age, but you always worked hard at what you loved. And look at you now." Their mother laughed. "Playing all the time!"

"Look at *him* now," Tiki grumbled, pointing to Ronde. "I'm sure I'll never run fast again. And football practice starts in two weeks."

Their mother paused. "Remember when you both tried out for the basketball team and didn't make it? You didn't quit then, did you?"

Tiki was silent.

"It's like I've always told you—believe in yourself and others will too," she said softly. "Wait. Wait and see."

Finally the doctor gave his orders: no more brace.

Tiki bent his knee back and forth.

"Go slow," the doctor said. "Take it easy."

"Let's go outside," Ronde whispered. Ronde took the old football out of the closet and passed it to his brother. It was the first football the twins had ever owned. A gift from their grandmother. It was rough now, scratched and worn. But it felt good in Tiki's hands.

They hurried downstairs and outside to the parking lot.

They warmed up, passing the ball back and forth.

"Go out," Ronde said. "I'll hit you."

Tiki moved gingerly on his stiff leg over the pavement. Ronde faded back, calling out, sounding like a sports announcer: "Ronde Barber looks for a receiver. He spots his brother near the ten-yard line."

"A perfect spiral. Bull's-eye! Caught by Tiki Barber." Tiki called back to his brother in his own announcer's voice. He waved the football over his head as both boys shouted at the same time, "Touchdown!"

Then September arrived. Tiki felt stronger and stronger. Football practice was every afternoon, even on the hottest days. But the boys didn't mind. They were teammates, together again.

Before practice Ronde and Tiki sat under the bleachers with their notebooks spread out. "Homework first," their mom always said. "It's not hard if you do a little every day."

Ronde worked on math, his favorite subject. Tiki read his history book. Sometimes he liked to dream of becoming an astronaut.

Finally a whistle sounded. The twins ran out with the others to the center of the green field. At practice they always ran everywhere. One of Coach Mike's favorite sayings was, "Only two people walk here—Coach Mike and the mailman!"

Everyone warmed up. Ronde jumped up and down. Tiki stretched his leg. So far so good. Today no one was wearing pads, and he felt so light on his feet. Yes, I can do it, Tiki told himself.

The offensive team practiced running wide, around the end. Tiki sprinted outside and tiptoed down the sideline. Again and again.

But just before practice was over, racing back, he slipped and fell.

Ronde was there first, looking down with a frightened gaze. "You all right?"

Tiki felt his leg. "Okay," he said, smiling. "Yeah, okay."

Ronde reached out a hand and pulled his brother up. Together they ran back to the huddle.

After practice they climbed to the top of the bleachers, waiting for their mom. Below them the field was empty.

Ronde looked down. "Do you ever think of us playing in a big stadium?" he asked Tiki. "In front of a great big crowd?"

"Really big?"

"Yeah. Super Bowl. Like that."

"That would be cool," Tiki said.

"Coach Mike says that if we—"

"I know. He told me. We have to keep working at it. Every day. Play our best."

"Know what I think?" Ronde asked his brother.

"What?" Tiki replied.

Ronde grinned and held up his hand. "Let's go for it!"

The twins high-fived just as they heard a car horn. They jumped down the wooden rows, two at a time, and raced to the car.

"What's up with you two?" their mom asked as they piled into the backseat.

"We were just talking."

"About?"

"Oh, about stuff. About becoming really, really good football players."

"Yeah. About even playing in the Super Bowl."

Their mother smiled as she started the car. "Well," she said. "Maybe. If you work hard enough."

Saturday morning . . . game time at last.

The twins' small faces stared out from underneath their helmets. Their mom was there, as always, watching. Cheering.

The boys looked up at their mother. "Give it your best," she said. "Don't forget. Play proud."

The opponents were going to kick off. The receiving team raced onto the field. Ronde and Tiki were farthest back, deep, side by side.

The kicker raised his hand. He moved forward with short steps.
The football soared high in the air, end over end.

"Yours," Ronde called out as Tiki circled beneath it. "Follow me. To the left.
All the way."

Tiki opened his arms and caught the ball. *Play proud.* He was racing now with Ronde just beside him—their feet flying over the grass.

Tiki and Ronde. Ronde and Tiki. Together.

All the way. Champions . . .

. . . brothers, side by side.